7 Bullets
Couldn't Kill Me

7 Bullets Couldn't Kill Me

"What comes at you in life doesn't have to take you out."

Jacob Lopez
Xulon Press

Xulon Press
2301 Lucien Way #415
Maitland, FL 32751
407.339.4217
www.xulonpress.com

Printed in the United States of America.

ISBN-13: 9781545610367

I dedicate this book to my wife Jamaira Lopez
and children Jericho and Abigail.

TO THE PEOPLE
WHO MADE ME WHO I AM TODAY:

To my parents Reverend Peter and Rosa Lopez, thank you for never speaking a negative word over my life and for your unconditional love. You will never be forgotten. To my second mother Nelly Dones, for being an inspiration and loving me as your own son.

TO MY BROTHER AND SISTER: Peter and Marilyn Lopez, thank you for your love and support.

TO WIFE AND CHILDREN: Jamaira, you are one of the strongest people I have ever known. Your love for God first is to be admired. I love how you have always been by my side. Jericho and Abigail thank you for being great kids through the ups and downs in our lives.

I ALSO WANT TO ACKNOWLEDGE: Bishop Joseph Andino, Dr. Adriana Mueller, Pastor Jonathan Soto, Pastor Pablo Pizarro, Pastor Charlie Cadiz, Pastor Kevin Scott, Pastor Eliseo Rivera, and Ricardo Pena for being a positive influence in my life and for always believing in me.

TO MY FAMILY AND FRIENDS: Thank you for always remembering me through my toughest time and for all your prayers.

I ALSO WANT TO ACKNOWLEDGE: James and Nora Orphanides, you have both been a tremendous blessing in my life and I am forever grateful for everything you have done for me and my family.

I ALSO WANT TO ACKNOWLEDGE: Dr. Larry Keefauver, thank you believing in my story and for all your help through this process and to the Xulon Press Team. You made it happen.

TO CHRIST ALONE: You are the only source of my life, thank you for being my Rock and Salvation. Your mercy has allowed me to live a tremendous life and now my story will never go untold.

Table of Contents

Introduction

How to Get the Most Out of This Book...

This book is my story. Each chapter is accompanied with five daily devotions to help you reflect, react and make the necessary changes in your spiritual journey.

Don't rush through this book in one swoop, let each chapter and devotion sink in and then apply the life lessons so that you are taking ownership of your life and using the authority God has given you to help you write your story.

Find the best time to read and apply the life lessons. If you're a morning person, set time aside in the mornings, maybe you like to eat good lunch and accompany it with a good book, well then use that time. If you're like me, maybe before you go to bed and have time to relax you might want to pick up this book. The important thing is that you pick up this book and read it.

This book will also challenge you during the weekend. As you rest, I also want you to reflect, worship and think about what you have read and how your life can change with God for the better.

Read on...

Week 1

Seven Bullets That Couldn't Kill Me

The Lord is my shepherd;
I shall not want.

He makes me to lie down in green pastures;
He leads me beside the still waters.

He restores my soul;
He leads me in the paths of righteousness
For His name's sake.

Yea, though I walk through the valley of the
shadow of death,
I will fear no evil;
For You are with me;
Your rod and Your staff, they comfort me.

You prepare a table before me in the presence of
my enemies;
You anoint my head with oil;
My cup runs over.

Surely goodness and mercy shall follow me
All the days of my life;
And I will dwell in the house of the Lord
Forever.
Psalm 23

Day 1 - *Facing Death at Point-Blank Range*

L ittle did I imagine that facing death was just moments away...

I was at our monthly gang meeting going over some projects. Then we headed out to a house party. When we got there, we were having a good time dancing, drinking, and smoking weed. One of the gang members came to tell me they were jumped by some drug dealers on Tremont Ave. Slim, gathered some soldiers to go make a statement to the other gang. We encountered the other fellas not knowing what was about to happen.

As we were approaching them, my gut feeling was this is going to end up ugly. Looking around, I noticed that our group had diminished in size down from fifteen guys to only four. My brain was screaming the thought, "I thought these guys were my boys that would have my back at all times. Where are they when I need them?" How quickly things change when you are facing an enemy.

I found myself alone with fifteen angry combatants from the enemy's side. Their leader shouted, "Who's your leader?" I shouted back, "I am." Immediately, he pulled out his gun and started shooting at me. I now wonder what would have happened if I had not been such a smart mouth and pointed out myself as the gang's leader. Would he have hesitated and not shot me or would it have made any difference? I had no time to react. Some of that moment when he began firing his gun is still blurry to me.

Fear seized me and all I knew to do was...*run!* I covered my face and turned my back trying to run and escape the bullets, but the guy kept shooting at me. Seven bullets slammed into my body as I fell to the ground and laid there dying in a pool of blood. After emptying his gun into me, my assailant walked away. One of my soldiers had a gun but never used it. I couldn't understand why he never used it and why no one else got into a fight while this was happening to me, I remember thinking, *Is this a setup? After all I had done for these "friends" and with the exception of one dude, all the rest had abandoned me.*

Situations like this one make one wonder who a person's true friends really are. I found myself alone with no one to help me. While I was laying on the ground bleeding to death, one of the guys who just stood there walked over to check on me. Because he was afraid of getting caught and get questioned by the cops, he didn't stay long. I now know the reality was that everyone was trying to save their own life. All of them fled the scene. Still, when you are part of a gang, you get sworn in and you vow that you will fight for one another. I was feeling very angry that they would leave me out in the cold. I began to scream, "Help, someone help me. I've been shot." Then I heard this lady from a nearby building screaming back at me, "Don't worry mijo; I called the ambulance and they should be on their way." I guess there is always someone watching, and at the same time happy she had done that.

Let me tell you, I learned over the years you've got to choose friends that are true to you. Just because another human being has vowed to protect you and even die for you, doesn't mean they have the courage or character when the going gets tough to really do it.

Think About This...

One of life's most important lessons is: **Choose the right friends.**

All of us have a need to belong. I thought that belonging to a gang would give me friends who had my back, would protect me, and friends that would be there for me even in the toughest of life's battles. I was prepared to die for my friends; but, I discovered they didn't have the same commitment to me. People will let you down, abandon you and even turn against you. One moment they can claim to be your BFF. In the next moment, they are running for their lives and you're lying on the ground bleeding out. Take to heart these words:

Oh, the joys of those who do not
follow the advice of the wicked,
or stand around with sinners,
or join in with mockers.
But they delight in the law of the Lord,
meditating on it day and night.
They are like trees planted along the riverbank,
bearing fruit each season.
Their leaves never wither,
and they prosper in all they do.
(Psalm 1:1-2 emphasis added)

Choose friends who are trustworthy and won't give you bad advice. Choose friends who tend to 'do the right thing' and do their best to live right.

Jesus said, *"Greater love has no one than this, than to lay down one's life for his friends"* (John 19:12). Yes, he proved Himself as a true, real BFF by dying for us. Choose to be with people that follow Jesus, the true friend who died for you and can be trusted when you face the "spiritual' bullets' that come your way.

- *Do you have any friends like that?*
- *Who would you die for?* (Make a list.)
- *Who would die for you as a true friend? Who can you trust?*

Learn this life lesson...say it and do it: ***I will choose the right friends beginning with Jesus.***

Day 2 - *Call 911*

The ambulance came like express delivery. The sound of the sirens were fading in and out. All of a sudden I found myself trying to answer the EMT who kept asking me what my name was. I was lying on the ground with almost no strength trying to mouth the words, "My name is Jacob." He kept telling me, "Don't close your eyes. Stay with us Jacob."

Just think for one second about where you are in life. You are doing well in life and all of a sudden you are facing death. Have you ever thought of the struggles you have gone through, and if it would not have been for God where would you be and what would be the end results?

I don't know the lady who called the ambulance, but I am grateful because if she hadn't I could have been dead in the streets and not being able to fulfill my dreams. But God had another plan for my life. We reached Lincoln Hospital; I heard nurses running towards the stretcher and rushing me to the operating room. It was like an action-suspense movie where everything becomes chaos because the doctors and nurses want to save your life. I had to undergo emergency surgery since I lost a lot of blood. I saw my life ending with despair and no hope. Looking back, what could have been the end for me became a new beginning. The same can be true for you. It depends how you view your future—with despair or hope. While all that was swirling around me at the hospital, I was hearing my father's voice say, "Call on the name of Jesus at all times, not only in the good but in the bad."

We often call on Him in times of need because when things are great who needs Jesus. That's how us humans think. Everyone tends to go on with their lives and everyday routine but it's in the times of trouble that God shows up and changes things for the good for them that trust Him and call out His name. Praise the name of Lord.

Think About This...

One of life's most important lessons is: *Call upon the Lord at all times.*

God says to each of us, *"Call upon me [the Lord] in the day of trouble; I shall rescue you, and you will honor me"* (Psalm 50:15). In my day of trouble, I trusted the wrong people to rescue me and it almost cost me my life. A stranger actually called for help and it came. Looking back, I believe that God rescued me then because He had a purpose for my life; He saved me.

Proverbs 20:22 reads, *"Do not say, "I will repay evil"; Wait for the LORD, and He will save you."* I don't blame the other guys in my gang for me getting shot. I had made some wrong choices and chosen to trust some bad people.

Learn this life lesson...say it and do it: *I will remember to call upon the name of the Lord at all times.*

Day 3 - *But God...*

I really don't remember in details what happened after the surgery or how my parents found out, what the cops were asking, or even who came to visit me. I don't recall because I went into a coma. I had complications from all the wounds and how my system was reacting. I knew this was going to be a long journey for me and my parents. I didn't want my parents to see me in this condition or for them to suffer for my wrong decisions. The process of recovery was going to be intense. I was in the Intensive Critical Care Unit with only limited visitations and I knew there were going to be people from all over trying to see me once the word was out.

However, my dad had to explain to the police they should have protection for me in case the other crew members found out I was in the hospital and would try to come finish the job completely. That was my father's mentality since he knew of the streets in his early age. As time went on, when I came out of a coma, I learned my dad, had asked a few members of the church to do a 24-hour prayer chain for me. My parents didn't waste any time and put their faith into action. They believed God would heal me, even in the midst of news they would receive from my doctors stating the opposite. Day in and day out, there were many people praying so that God would have His way during this process. The nurses and doctors where amazed at how my parents were declaring scriptures over my life and singing songs of praise and worship as they waited and waited for the outcome.

It was a tough time for everyone. It's crazy how my father found the Bible he gave me in my back pocket in my pants. He was surprised that after all my rebellion and running away from family and God that I would still carry it with me. He didn't think I would read it, but truth be told, I did when I was alone.

Yes, I had made wrong decisions and chose some bad folks to hang with. I truly believe God was watching over me at all times. During all of that time in my life of being out on the streets, I never was caught by an officer, which is rare since you are running the streets with drugs. I think about it today and I have to say, "But God...."

But God was there for me when I wasn't there for Him.
But God didn't give up on me.
But God didn't leave or forsake me.
But God kept me alive when I didn't deserve it.

Think About This...

One of life's most important lessons is: **God will never leave or forsake you.**

I had known about God and the Bible for years. I put my trust in the wrong people and it almost lost my life because of it. Truth is, God's good plan and purpose would have been cut short if I had died there on the street. *But God* had put good parents and people around me who didn't give up on me. I discovered that God really meant it when He said,

"I will never leave you or forsake you."
(Hebrews 13:5)

It doesn't matter how far you run away from God, He's always right there for you. Stop making wrong choices. Turn away from bad advice and evil people. Turn back to God. The moment you do, you'll discover He's had your back all the time.

Learn this life lesson...say it and do it: *God never leaves or forsakes me.*

Day 4 - *Own Your Decisions and Their Consequences*

K nowing I was shot at close range, the doctors knew it was a high-risk surgery because the bullets penetrated my stomach. Other slugs were found in both my thighs, but the doctors were amazed because none of my organs were damaged. I survived the surgery, responding to the medication, and my vital signs kept getting stronger. I kept thinking to myself how grateful I was to God that He had spared my life.

There are choices you have to make in life choosing the right path and try not to get caught up with foolish things that sometimes delay your journey. You may ask yourself or others, "Why does God allow bad things to happen." I don't have that answer for you but I do know that we will suffer the consequences for bad choices. It's goes back to the choices we make. They're either going to get us into trouble and send us down the wrong path or launch us into our purpose. We think we know better than God, and He lets us make our own decisions even though we see all the signs that say, *Danger!*

God does give us hints to avoid temptations and to stay away from bad advice given by wicked people, but we ignore the warning signs. God is a gentleman. He will not force Himself on anyone. I knew what I was doing on the streets was wrong; all the warning signs were there to keep me from danger, but I chose to ignore them and

I suffered the consequences. When I woke up from my coma, I was told some of my crew came and told my dad that they wanted to get revenge for what happened to me. They would find out who had shot me and make the guilty parties pay. My dad without hesitation, told them God was fighting on our behalf, that we will trust Him to work out the rest.

After what seemed to be like a year but in reality was one very long month, I was discharged from the hospital to start the recovering process. I had a choice to make, either I went back to the life I had prior to getting shot or to disconnect from the gang life. I chose to disconnect and not only heal physically but also spiritually. Plus I didn't want to have my parents in any type of danger. I must confess that anger began to arise within me. Yes, at times I wanted to take matters into my own hands and go get the person that had shot me. I didn't want God to fight on my behalf. I remember one night just laying in the bed being totally dependent on my parents taking care of me and having all these feeling of revenge overcome me that I couldn't sleep. That was not an easy process. I had prided myself in being an independent person. I kept asking myself, "Why did this happen?" You know, your mind and heart will play tricks on you, right? I couldn't sleep and when I could I had nightmares.

I discovered that choosing the wrong path, just to have friends and be popular in the street life, had brought terrible consequences into my life. After a while, my dad told me to go stay with close family friends in New Jersey until everything subsided. I had to get away from the area where the gangs were. The enemy of my soul began to play with my thoughts and feelings. I was distraught and confused. It was hard to think clearly. I found myself in a dark place. Physically, I couldn't walk properly so I had to go for rehab for a few months. I had a terrible limp that would not go away and pain constantly shooting all through my leg. It was painful. Also, because of all the meds that I had to take, I had lost my appetite and felt depressed. My injury also took me away from playing sports and from normal day to day things. I realize now how important my decisions are and how they not only affect me but also those around me.

Think About This...

One of life's most important lessons is: **Own your decisions. Confess what you've done wrong and your darkness will turn to light!**

I needed to discover the truth of this passage:

"This is the message we heard from Jesus and now declare to you: God is light, and there is no darkness in him at all. So, we are lying if we say we have fellowship with God but go on living in spiritual darkness; we are not practicing the truth. But if we are living in the light, as God is in the light, then we have fellowship with each other, and the blood of Jesus, his Son, cleanses us from all sin. **"If we claim we have no sin, we are only fooling ourselves and not living in the truth. But if we confess our sins to him, he is faithful and just to forgive us our sins and to cleanse us from all wickedness.** *If we claim we have not sinned, we are calling God a liar and showing that his word has no place in our hearts."*
(1 John 1:5-10 NLT)

Are you in a dark place because of some wrong decisions or hanging out with the wrong people? Get away from those people. I had to do that; so do you. Get out of a dark place full of despair and depression. Instead, confess what you've done wrong and get cleaned up by God. That will move you from darkness to light.

Learn this life lesson...say this and do this: *I confess my sins, accept His forgiveness, and start walking in the light.*

Day 5 - *Break Old Habits*

New Jersey became my new home. I stayed with a family member named Charlie. He opened his home and told me to stay as long as I needed to. I was happy I was able to do that. I wanted to be closer to my parents but that couldn't happen just yet. I kept having nightmares reliving the moment I was shot; it was hard to deal with the real world on a daily basis. My mind was torturing me; at one point, I thought I was going to lose my mind. Fear became the norm. For example, I was constantly looking over my shoulder, even when I was alone. It was the worst feeling and made it hard to trust again. As the days would go from day light to night, I starting to put up a wall and didn't want to get close to anyone. Fear was trying to paralyze me from moving forward.

I understand now that when we hold on to hurt, after a while, that hurt becomes hate, then hate gets in the way for us to love and trust, then before we know it we become bitter. Are we going to wait or are we going to deal with the root cause of what we are faced with? Will we continue to ignore it, or with a sincere heart, surrender it to God?

Old habits are hard to break. Yet, I had positive, God-fearing people who would help me in prayer and who allowed me to go through my process in life. I wasn't judged or rushed into doing anything I wasn't ready to do.

The crazy part of this is that as life when on, years later I had the opportunity to get married. One day my wife had noticed I was limping and not walking as my normal self. She asked me if I was okay when I said it's just some pain in my leg. She asked if she could see the leg when she felt a bump and saw that a bullet was pressing out of my leg. We tried to squeeze it out but it wouldn't come out. I went to my doctor because I didn't want to get an infection or make matters worse and because it started to cause me a lot of pain. My doctor couldn't believe that after so long the bullet would work its way out of my body. He used some equipment and squeezed the area of the bullet, that bullet flew out. I was bugging out and so was my doctor. Now I understood why I was having pain but never had felt the bullet pressing against my skin.

Years ago, I had to make a decision to walk in the light and not in darkness. I learned from Proverbs 20:22, *"Do not say, 'I will recompense evil'; Wait for the LORD, and He will save you."* Then I discovered Romans 12:19, *"Do not take revenge, my dear friends, but leave room for God's wrath, for it is written: 'It is mine to avenge; I will repay,' says the Lord."* It also goes on to say, *"Do not give the devil a foothold."* I decided to let go of my hurt and hate and move away from darkness to light. To start moving into the direction God had for me instead of dwelling in the past. That took time and it was a long process but one that I'm so grateful for now.

Today, learn this life lesson...say this and do this: *I will not let the past determine my future. God's plans for me are good!*

At the End of This Week...

Take a couple of days and write down a few things you have learned this week:

- *About Yourself...*
- *About God...*
- *About one way you need to change...*

Week 2 -

Are Bullets Chasing You or Are You Chasing the Cross?

⸻

In our culture, success is based on achievement. We admire those who perform well in business. However, greatness in God's Kingdom is found in a life of obedience in the Cross. Here are some questions to ask yourself. Are you following His plan and helping others as Jesus did? Have you shared with others the Good News of Christ or are you still chasing bullets? You choose, you decide.

Sometimes people choose the wrong path knowing the right direction which can lead to destruction, stress, frustration, and instability. Many of us have made

Sometimes people choose the wrong path knowing the right direction which can lead to destruction, stress, frustration, and instability.

some mistakes that have caused setbacks in our lives because we haven't made a decision to learn from them. We keep stumbling around the same issues because we haven't surrendered it to God. It's our fault because God is always giving us a solution on how we can overcome these circumstances but we tend to choose the wrong door. I am thankful that God gave me a second chance to get my life right this time and that I was able to exit thought the right door since I was on my way to death.

This week we will discover how to turn a broken lock with the only key that can work?

Day 1 - *The Key to the Rest of Your Life*

Living a life in Christ is living free of sin, of past mistakes, wrong choices, bad decisions, and destructive behaviors. Dodging those bullets shot out of the gun of making bad decisions to gain life through the Cross of Christ begins with making a decision to follow Christ.

Will you let past bullets of wrong decisions shoot down and kill your present and more importantly your future dreams—the purposes and possibilities that God has for you? The key to your future is the decision to follow Jesus Christ.

Take a bullet or dodge one, the choice is yours. Those destructive bullets from the past represent darkness, failure, confusion, anger, and hatred at the end of the road. Don't follow or chase after those past bullets, chase after the Cross and gain Jesus. The bullets of past mistakes and bad choices are like our old nature which needs to be crucified. Our old ways of thinking need God's truths so that our minds can be renewed. We need to die, to be crucified to our misbeliefs and the lies of the past and be changed by the truths of God—we have the mind of Christ.

Reflect on your past for a minute and see what it looked like to how your present is. Remember how lost you were in your mess. Recall when you thought no one was there to help you and you felt alone. The great news is that God was there waiting for you to call on Him. Are you chasing the Cross which can heal your pain or letting the bullets from past sin chase you down and kill your dreams? Many of us want to chase fame which can always lead to destruction because of our pride. Remember, the choices we make today will determine where we going tomorrow.

Think About This...

Starting over and changing begins at the Cross. Paul writes in Galatians 2:20, "*I have been crucified with Christ and I no longer live, but Christ lives in me. The life I live in the body, I live by faith in the Son of God, who loved me and gave himself for me*" (NIV).

Make a list of all your past mistakes that still gun you down in your present decisions, actions, feelings, and thoughts. Repent, surrender them now, nail them to the Cross of Christ.

Learn this life lesson...say this and do this: **My past is crucified with Christ; I live a new life in Christ.**

Day 2 - *Make Right Decisions*

I want to encourage you to start making better decisions. It's easier for us to make bad choices then to do what's right. Are you struggling with areas you don't want help in? Are you too prideful to reach out like Peter who was sinking and cried out, "Lord, save me"?

Let me assure you that the Almighty is there to lift us up and will always love us no matter how many wrongdoings are piled up from our past mistakes and failures. We tend to just hold on to these strongholds that won't allow us to be free and so we continue to kill our own visions and dreams. We won't be able to see the greater picture unless we let go completely. The time is now. Decide to let go of the things that tear you down. Don't think you are too late because you are not, God is telling you that He is here to wipe away all of your sins and cleanse you with his precious blood.

Choose today to make the change that is needed in your life. Change happens when you embrace the truth, so embrace His truth and be free. Jesus confirms that *"...you shall know the truth and the truth will set you free"* (John 8:32). Josh McDowell in *Right From Wrong"* reminds us that absolute truth is true all the time, for all people, and in all situations. However, most of us base our decisions on myths or half-truths. These are often called conventional or human wisdom. A myth is what's right for some people, in some situations, some of the time.

Such relativism will become a bullet of destruction for you. Absolute truth found in Jesus Christ—the way, the truth, and the life—is the only key that will unlock your God's forgiving love and your unlimited potential in Christ.

Think About This...

You have the mind of Christ, the Scriptures, and the power to make right decisions based on absolute truth instead of the relativism of myths, lies, and half-truths propagated all around you by culture. Will you choose truth over comfort or fear? Will you do what's right instead of what's convenient?

Learn this life lesson...say this and do this: **Jesus Christ is the truth; the truth sets me free.**

Day 3 - *Can't Change Your Past, So Change Your Future*

Your past doesn't determine your future. Your past may have been shaped by a number of different factors and influences. Many of us are a product from our community. We are all identified by our family blood line. Sometimes we based our excuses where we came from like *'my father wasn't there, my mother was always busy, I never had a brother to defend me,'* and the list goes on and on. You can live this way forever not knowing your future, hope, and purpose.

The old bullets in your life can be buried once and for all. God tells you in Isaiah 43:18-19, *"Forget the former things; do not dwell in the past. See, I am doing a new thing! Now it springs forth, do you not see perceive it?"* Then Paul writes in 2 Corinthians 5:17, *"For Christ's love compels us, because we are convinced that one died for all, and therefore all died. And he died for all, that those who live should no longer live for themselves but for him who died for them and was raised again. So, from now on we regard no one from a worldly point of view. Though we once regarded Christ in this way, we do so no longer. Therefore, if anyone is in Christ, he is a new creation; the old has gone, the new has come!"* (2 Corinthians 5:14-17 NIV).

> *Your past doesn't determine your future.*

So, how do you move beyond who you've been and become a new creation? The answer is easy, God's love changes everything. Your past is wiped clean of dirt, sin, mistakes, failures, and wrong choices. Scripture promises that His perfect love eradicates all fear and forgives all sin.

Unlocking your future begins with love, *"I urge you, therefore, to reaffirm your love to him. The reason I wrote you was to see if you would stand the test and be obedient in everything"* (2 Corinthians 2:8-9). Right now, start fresh. Receive Christ's love from the Cross for yourself; and, reaffirm your love for Him.

Think About This...

Stop dwelling in the past. The past doesn't determine your present or your future unless you let it. The bullets of your past failures can't gun you down unless you continue to make yourself a target! Change begins with love. So, reaffirm your love for Christ now!

Learn this life lesson...say this and do this: **Christ's love makes me a new person!**

Day 4 - *Transformed! Changed!*

I was in a gang. My life was a mess. However, the truth is that God changed me and He can change you. I know that anyone with a willing heart can be transformed by God because I am a living witness. I have learned with Paul (Romans 7) that I have the desire to do what is good, but I cannot carry it out most of the time. We do what's good when needed, but evil is always present.

Now if I do what is right, it's not to be high and mighty but to live free from my doubt, fear, and past guilt. Most of us have the potential achieve many great goals in life but we come up with excuses. Sometimes we try to move forward, but fear steps in and remind us about our past. Remember what I just wrote from the Scriptures, *"Perfect love casts out fear"* (1 John 4:18).

Fear is a weapon that Satan uses to get full access in our life, but when you have the assurance of God's love for you, you can't be defeated. In His love for us, God smashes to smithereens all fear. Renew your mind with this truth, *"For God has not given us a spirit of fear, but of power and of love and of a sound mind"* (2 Timothy 1:7).

Think About This...

Know the devices of your enemy—Satan. His greatest weapon against you is fear—fear of past guilt catching up with you; fear of failure; fear of making a mistake; and the fear of surrender...letting go. Refuse to take the bullet of fear. Instead, receive from God's spirit his gifts of love, power, and a sound mind.

Learn this life lesson...say this and do this: **God has given me a spirit of power, love, and a sound mind.**

Day 5 - *Stop Living a Double life*

If any of you lacks wisdom, he should ask God,
who gives generously to all without finding fault,
and it will be given to him.
But when he asks, he must believe and not doubt,
because he who doubts is like a wave of the sea,
blown and tossed by the wind.
That man should not think he will receive anything from
the Lord;
he is a double-minded man, unstable in all he does.
(James 1:5-8 NIV)

Holding on to our dead, destructive past while also trying to grasps God's wonderful, limitless future for us is simply being "double-mind." In the movie, *Catch Me If You Can,* we see one of the most notorious double lives in recent history. The film is a biographical narrative based on the life of Frank Abagnale, who conned scores of people and companies and scammed millions of dollars by the age of nineteen by living the double life of a pilot, doctor, and prosecuting attorney. But, he changed and became a renowned agent for the FBI helping the Bureau catch forgers and con-artists. How much longer are we going to continue to hold on to that heavy baggage? Frank Abagnale proved that you can best recognize a fake by knowing the original.

Stop living a fake life and get to know the perfect, original, and unique person in all of history—Jesus Christ. Stop lugging around the past; get rid of your baggage just like Frank Abagnale did of trading a life in prison for a new life living the truth.

An elephant can weigh as much as 24,000 pounds and reach heights of 13 feet tall. Its trunk is strong enough to rip branches from trees, but despite their enormous power, elephants can be chained. When you consider this, it is hard to believe that such a powerful animal can be chained and confined. When an elephant is young, all it takes is a small chain fastened to a metal collar around the elephant's foot to be attached by a wooden nail. This holds the elephant so strongly that it can't break free. As an adult, all the huge elephant knows is the memory of being unable to break the chain on his foot as a baby. So, he believes the myth or lie that he cannot break free of his chains as an adult.

As adults, we allow ourselves to be bound by the chains of our past. As Christians, we often live double lives of being chained and imprisoned by the strongholds of our past. We choose to be confined and even comfortable in our chains instead of breaking free into God's purposes and potential for us. We tend to get comfortable and don't acknowledge change very well. We feel like everything has gone wrong so how can things get any better and we lose hope.

God is glorified in the situations when we seize the lifeline of his truth and break free of the shackles of the past. He sees our pain and always shows up to fight for us and on our behalf. He doesn't lose hope to see us transformed and renewed from our bondages.

This whole week, we have been looking at the bullets that take us down. Here's a final one for you to reflect on. Stop making a habit of repeating the past. That's called habitual sin which certainly displeases God.

In James 4:7 we are told, *"Resist the devil, and he will flee from you."* Often in trials we face in our lives are the work of the enemy. We cry out to God for help in our circumstances. When we resist the enemy, and use the authority of Jesus Christ, we have power to decide to be renewed in our minds instead of letting the dark side of this world trick you. Take a stand against all that comes your way rather its sickness, loneliness, sadness or despair. Once you resist, the dark powers will flee from you. Evil will exist because we permit it.

Matthew 16:16 reads, *"Verily I say unto you, Whatever ye shall bind on earth shall be bound in heaven: and whatever ye loose on earth shall be loosed in heaven."* Exercise your authority on earth because we have no defeat in heaven. What will you believe, your truth or God's truth? Your truth says, you can't make it but God's truth says you shall make it. Your truth says, you won't get healed but Gods truth says, you are healed. Today is your day to live and choose the bullet or the cross.

At the End of This Week…

Take a couple of days and write down a few things you have learned this week:

- *About Yourself…*
- *About God…*
- *About one way you need to change…*

Week 3 -

The Letter of Death

In the spring, at the time when kings go off to war, David sent Joab out with the king's men and the whole Israelite army. They destroyed the Ammonites and besieged Rabbah. But David remained in Jerusalem. ² One evening David got up from his bed and walked around on the roof of the palace. From the roof he saw a woman bathing. The woman was very beautiful, ³ and David sent someone to find out about her. The man said, "She is Bathsheba, the daughter of Eliam and the wife of Uriah the Hittite." ⁴ Then David sent messengers to get her. She came to him, and he slept with her. (Now she was purifying herself from her monthly uncleanness.) Then she went back home. ⁵ The woman conceived and sent word to David, saying, "I am pregnant."

⁶ So David sent this word to Joab: "Send me Uriah the Hittite." And Joab sent him to David. ⁷ When Uriah came to him, David asked him how Joab was, how the soldiers were and how the war was going. ⁸ Then David said to Uriah, "Go down to your house and wash your feet." So Uriah left the palace, and a gift from the king was sent after him. ⁹ But Uriah slept at the entrance to

the palace with all his master's servants
and did not go down to his house.
[10] David was told, "Uriah did not go home." So he asked
Uriah, "Haven't you just come from a military
campaign? Why didn't you go home?"
[11] Uriah said to David, "The ark and Israel and Judah are
staying in tents, and my commander Joab and my lord's
men are camped in the open country. How could I go to
my house to eat and drink and make love to my wife?
As surely as you live, I will not do such a thing!"
[12] Then David said to him, "Stay here one more day, and
tomorrow I will send you back." So Uriah remained in
Jerusalem that day and the next. [13] At David's invitation,
he ate and drank with him, and David made him drunk.
But in the evening Uriah went out to sleep on his mat
among his master's servants; he did not go home.
[14] In the morning David wrote a letter to Joab and sent
it with Uriah. [15] In it he wrote, "Put Uriah out in front
where the fighting is fiercest. Then withdraw from him
so he will be struck down and die." (2 Samuel 11:1-15)

Covering up sin creates more darts the enemy can use to put us down and destroy our destiny. This story is filled with the devices the enemy uses to destroy God's potential and provision in our lives.

Day 1 - *The Bullet of "Being in the Wrong Place...Doing the Wrong Thing"*

David was a King and kings were known to fight wars, lead armies, and protect their people. From verse 1, we learn that one day, David didn't do what he was purposed and created to do as a king. Whenever we are not fulfilling God's plan for our lives, we will find ourselves open to the enemy's attack. Such was the case with David.

When we are not doing God's work and following His lead, we are opening ourselves to all kinds of temptations. Consider this:

"For all that is in the world — the lust of the flesh, the lust of the eyes, and the pride of life — is not of the Father but is of the world. And the world is passing away, and the lust of it; but he who does the will of God abides forever."
(1 John 2:16-17)

The bullet that shot David was like buckshot—the consequence of him not doing God's will led David into many different, deadly sins. Not only did he commit adultery with Bathsheba, but he also planned the murder of Uriah.

Think About This...

Before making any ethical or moral decision, ask yourself, "What will be the good or bad consequence of my decision be?"

Learn this life lesson...say this and do this: **I refuse to follow the lust of my flesh or eyes or my pride; I will follow Jesus.**

Day 2 - *What Letter Do You Carry?*

W e are told in Scripture that David sent a letter with Uriah to give to Joab. All Uriah knew was that he was carrying a letter from the King to one of his Commanders; he had no idea that this letter was a blacklist and his name was the only one on it. What letter are you carrying? What do others say about you? What is God's will for your life?

The devil was trying to take me out. I was marked for death but God intervened. Adam chose to do what he wanted instead of what God wanted. Every selfish choice

he had no idea that this letter was a blacklist and his name was the only one on it.

leads us to destruction. What does the letter of your life say? Is it one that pleases God or seeks to please men? How does your letter read?

"You are our epistle written in our hearts, known and read by all men; clearly you are an epistle of Christ, ministered by us, written not with ink but by the Spirit of the living God, not on tablets of stone but on tablets of flesh, that is, of the heart." (2 Corinthians 3:2-3)

Think About This...

Your life is an open book for all to read. What does it say of you? Are the chapters more about you than God?

Who has the leading role? Who is writing your story?

Think of each day filled with appointments written in the pencil of God's will. You have a permanent ink pen and eraser. You can rewrite God's will for each moment in life in the permanent ink of your surrender—following Jesus. Or, you can erase what He wants and write into each day what you desire. When you flip through the diary of the pages of your life, is most of it written in the permanent ink of His shed blood on the Cross for you, or have you chosen to write in pencil which fades and washes away in the temporary wants of your selfish choices?

Learn this life lesson...say this and do this: **My life is a living letter written about Christ not about me!**

Day 3 - *Where Are You Headed?*

U riah thought he was headed to battle to fight for
his King. However, King David was sending Uriah
to die. So, who can you trust with the direction of your
life? Those around you? It's sad but true that even those
closest to you can let you down or betray you. Only God
can direct your steps so that you finish strong, finish right,
and finish victorious.

You can be a man marked for death but God has the
last word. Many of us worry so much on "why" that we
never focus on the word "what." We must ask "What does
God require of me?" instead of "Why, does this happen?"

We always ask the question why! You may be reading
this and saying the same thing. Why did I allow myself to
open up? Why did I go out that night? Why did I open the
door while my parents were gone? Let's change the *why*
to *what*: *What can I do to serve the King of kings.*

The mighty man, Uriah, died because of his faithfulness
to King David. He would never open the letter because of
his loyalty to the King. The same way he was loyal, we
need to be loyal to God. He died with no shame, and that
made King David's sin greater. Does that make sense? I
rather die for truth then to live a lie.

You can have moments when you are feeling down but
God is there to lift you up. Your worst days will be better
days, even your dark nights will become brighter. Many of
us are carrying that letter of death but even through your

suffering, great things can occur. We will never know how amazing God is until we go through some tough moments. Let's make that change, while we are alive.

Think About This...

Do you have a letter from the past that speaks death into your life today? Maybe someone hurt you, gossiped about you, or even tried to physically hurt you. Have you forgiven them? Have you shared Jesus with them? What kind of letter are you writing back to them?

Learn this life lesson...say this and do this: **I want to write a love letter from Christ to others with my life.**

Day 4 - *Wherein Does Your Loyalty Lie?*

Think about it. I was loyal to my gang and in one night everything changed. I remember like it was yesterday. I dropped to the floor and felt my spirit and soul separating from my body. Blood gushing out all over. As I saw the street spinning around, I could feel the holy hand of God taking me by the hand and holding me. I heard Him say He was the faithful author of life sustaining me the whole time, even when my enemies were laughing at me.

How can we relate to this story? Have we played the role of David, Bathsheba, and Uriah? Think about that?

David was known as King David, King over Israel, the man after God's heart, the shepherd boy who fought lions, bears, and took down Goliath. Let's view this with a different perspective. We think that the trials we face always come from the devil. Not true...sometimes God allows it.

David committed adultery all on his own. Yes, he was tempted but the devil didn't make him do it or if he had gone out to do battle as he was supposed to, he would not have set himself up for failure. Evil took its course based on his wrongful decision; David had no one else to blame but himself.

Think About This...

What past decisions do you need to take responsibility for? When will you stop blaming the devil or others for your own mistakes? Who are you loyal to—yourself, another person, or only to Christ?

Learn this life lesson...say this and do this: **I will take responsibility for my own thoughts, feeling, and action and stop blaming others.**

Day 5 - *Who Does God Love the Most?*

M aybe you are having a bad day. Let me remind you, God loves you even when you are making wrong decisions. God loved David. God could identify with both men like David and Uriah. In the New Testament, we learn that Jesus was also betrayed. David had a grace period to repent immediately but he didn't. Many of us are in a season of spiritual trouble. We start the journey strong with Jesus but as life goes on, we want to give up more times than not. We start well and lose the spark; at times, we lose faith. God stands by to watch, desiring for us to learn from our wrong doings. It's sad when hurting people hurt people but it's true, hurting people hurt people! It's what they know to do. All I can tell you is that even if you lose faith and give up on God, others or yourself, God will never give up on you.

In your mother's womb, the Lord knew you. God's intention is to help you forgive yourself and others even as He has forgiven you. Remember Philippians 1:6 written by Paul: *"He (God in Christ) who began a good work in you will carry it on to completion until the day of Jesus Christ."* We know Uriah died in vain, but his death will never go unnoticed. Let's choose today what can we do to live better and write an excellent letter for Christ with our lives.

JACOB LOPEZ

At the End of This Week...

Take a couple of days and write down a few things you have learned this week:

- *About Yourself...*
- *About God...*
- *About one way you need to change...*

Week 4 -

The Power of Prayer

What is intercessory prayer? It's praying for others and others praying for you.

Who are you praying for?
Who is praying for you?

L eonard Ravenhill wrote, "To be much for God, we must be much with God. Jesus, that lone figure in the wilderness, knew strong crying, along with tears. Can one be moved with compassion and not know tears? Jeremiah was a sobbing saint. Jesus wept! So, did Paul. So, did John. Though there are some tearful intercessors behind the scenes, I grant you that to our modern Christianity, praying is foreign."[1] Scripture urges us to "pray for one another" (James 5:16).

A speaker once asked, "Who hasn't been healed because we have not prayed? Who has been lost because we failed to pray? Who still languishes in the chains of bondage and suffering because we have not prayed?' Someone is waiting on the other side of your obedience to the mandate of intercession. When will you pray?

Day 1 - *Stand in the Gap*

A s a believer, we owe it to another to always stand in the gap to pray for one another. God sorrowfully comments in Ezekiel 22:30, *"So I sought for a man among them who would make a wall, and stand in the gap before Me on behalf of the land, that I should not destroy it; but I found no one."* Have you even been too busy today, but prompted in the midst of all your rushing to stop and pray? The work of intercession is never an interruption. It is an invitation to open up the doors of heaven's mercy and grace upon someone who desperately needs your prayers today.

No matter how short the prayer is, standing in the gap in prayer for others is a powerful weapon against the enemy and an amazing shield of protection. According to some dictionaries, standing in the gap in prayer means *to expose one's self for the protection of something; to make defense against any assailing danger; to take the place of fallen defender or supporter.*

When you pray for others, you call God Almighty on their behalf. It can be asking God to have mercy on them, to give them increased wisdom, strength, and grace. It can also be a prayer of divine protection from the devices of the evil one. We have heard many testimonies of people who received salvation because their grandmother, parents, and friends stood in the gap in prayer for God to show them his love. Many lives have been saved from destruction, sickness, and disease because someone somewhere was praying for them.

Think About This...

Make an intercession list of people and their needs. Keep a prayer journal. Decide to stand in the gap and intercede for others.

Learn this life lesson...say it and do it: **I will be a daily intercessor in prayer for others.**

Day 2 - *Pray Don't Condemn*

Discernment is God's call to intercession, never to faultfinding.
-Corrie Ten Boom

Many people today focus on condemning others instead of praying and standing in the gap for them. We deal with so much as children growing up, such as being bullied, mistreated, or lied to just to name a few. Many secretly contemplate suicide to cope with depression. They seek for quick answers to help them feel good instead of dealing with root causes to their problem.

God's promise is that if we draw near to Him, He will draw near to us. Life is a gift from God, and only He knows our expiration date here on this side of heaven. Many people say troubles do not last all day, because joy comes in the morning. But many don't know the hell you been through before the morning even came, like no food in the fridge to feed your kids. I remember waiting on the line for cheese, milk with my mother on a cold snowy days. She would always look at my eyes and tell me, "Better days are coming, son. We will have many cold nights but this won't last forever. Your prosperous days will surpass dry seasons. The open heaven will never close its resources, when I am gone. What I have taught you will take its course."

Most of the time I didn't understand my mother's words of wisdom because I was very young, however, I always felt she was speaking to my destiny. I truly believe "God doesn't talk to people who don't talk to him". My mother Rose Lopez walked and lived by this amazing scripture (Matthew 6:6) *But when you pray, go into your room, close the door and pray to your Father, who is unseen. Then your Father, who sees what is done in secret, will reward you.* Yes, I was the black sheep of the family. I did the opposite until opposition arose in my times of trouble. I often think, 'what if my mother never prayed for me.' I know without a shadow of a doubt that her prayers in secret paid off publicly in my life. Yes, times were tough nothing was given to us. We had to make it work. If you're reading this and you're a parent, please don't give up on your children because they are not living your standards. Maybe your daughter's marriage didn't work or they ended up in prison. Our responsibility is to pray for them and love them right where they are. You think Jesus would stop praying for them?

Think About This...

Learn this life lesson...say it and do it: **I will not use my words to condemn. I will use my words to love, build and encourage.**

Day 3 - *Intercede for Our Nation*

I n the world we live in today full of chaos that can't be ignored, it's sad that many of our students in America are being expelled or end up arrested, in gangs, or prisons, in foster homes, and the list goes on. After the prayers were taken out of our schools, many YMCAs were also removed from many communities. Prayer was a stabilizing factor in our schools, communities, and government institutions which brought some harmony, peace, and respect among our citizens. "Can we change that?" Let me share more insight on how believers can pray effectively for others who are in need of help. God says this:

"If My people who are called by My name will humble themselves, and pray and seek My face, and turn from their wicked ways, then I will hear from heaven, and will forgive their sin and heal their land. Now My eyes will be open and My ears attentive to prayer made in this place."
(2 Chronicles 7:14)

Let's learn how to stand in the gap with intercessory prayer. Our prayers will bridge the gap between God and our nation. When need to stand in the gap with prayer. We need to pray and ask for God's help, mercy, intervention, and forgiveness. We need to pray on behalf of individuals and groups of people who are so bound and broken that

JACOB LOPEZ

they can't pray for themselves. We need to pray in the Spirit even when we don't know what to pray for in the natural. Prayer changes things. Let's bring forth change with prayer.

Think About This...

Learn this life lesson...say it and do it – **I will stand in the gap through prayer for my Nation.**

Day 4 - *Pray in One Accord*

W e need to be in one accord as the early Christian's in Acts Chapter 1 were. We must stand in the gap for one another. Pray for those who are in critical situations, who don't know Jesus, who may not know how to pray or who don't even believe in the power of prayer. Stop praying for changed circumstances; pray for inner change. Prayer is a weapon and it transforms us to have the mind of Christ.

Praying in agreement and unity begins in the home. Husbands and wives, parents and children, need to pray in agreement. Making Christ the center of our home and spending a few minutes in prayer together will impact families. Jesus teaches us, *"Again I say to you that if two of you agree on earth concerning anything that they ask, it will be done for them by My Father in heaven. For where two or three are gathered together in My name, I am there in the midst of them."* (Matthew 18:19-21)

If we're not careful, our prayers can be very selfish. For example, if your prayers are God, change my spouse, my boss, teacher or situation just because we are unhappy and are not willing to go through the process that will change and make us better, that those prayers are more for you than them. Our prayers should be more of a time of thanksgiving, asking God to help us die to our flesh so we could be more like Him. Stop agreeing with flesh and blood and start agreeing with God. When we agree with God for His will in our lives then heaven does come to earth and anything is possible in His divine plan and purpose.

Think About This...

Are you ready to stop insisting on your way and begin to desire and agree with God's will and way? God is saying to you as you intercede:

> *"For My thoughts are not your thoughts,*
> *Nor are your ways My ways," says the Lord.*
> *"For as the heavens are higher than the earth,*
> *So are My ways higher than your ways,*
> *And My thoughts than your thoughts.*
> *(Isaiah 55:8-9)*

In your intercession for others, begin to pray His will over your family, friends, colleagues at work or school, as well as for your church and nation.

List those you are interceding for and then pray this: Our Father who are in heaven, hallowed be Your name, Your kingdom come, Your will be done in the lives of

_____

_____

Learn this life lesson...say it and do it: **I will intercede and pray for God's will in my life and in the lives of others.**

Day 5 - *Prayer Opens the Door for God to Change Us and Others*

As we pray, the doors of heaven open up and God's Spirit is poured out on the lives of people, institutions, and nations. Intercession invites God to enter into our thoughts, feelings, and actions to transform what's negative to that which is positive and to transform impossibilities into possibilities.

Never stop praying against injustice, government and legal institutions that are corrupt. If God's people pray, God's Spirit begins to work in them and through them to bring about His renewal and change. Intercede for others—suicide, addiction, abuse, depression, anger, and violence are plaguing our society. Remember the hope that God brings to us when He says, *"If my people, who are called by my name, will humble themselves and pray and seek my face and turn from their wicked ways, then I will hear from heaven, and I will forgive their sin and will heal their land."*

In what areas of your life do you need to humble yourself and begin interceding right now to God? Take a minute to write down a prayer of repentance:

_____

_____

_____

At the End of This Week...

Take a couple of days and write down a few things you have learned this week:

- *About Yourself...*
- *About God...*
- *About the way you need to change...*

Week 5 -

Born to Live

Many of us don't know our purpose in life. Do most of us even value the day we entered into this world? Sometimes we ask, "Why are we here?" Our minds are riddled with self-doubts and many questions. Do I belong to this family? Why do I even exist? Our cry from the depths of our heart is, "Lord, why am I here? What is my purpose?" Rick Warren, Author of the Bestselling Book, *The Purpose Driven Life,* writes,

"If you are alive,
There's a purpose for your life."

The preacher who wrote the ancient book of Ecclesiastes declares,

To everything there is a season,
A time for every purpose under heaven.
(Ecclesiastes 3:1)

The Hebrew word for "purpose" is *chaplets* which is also translated "desire" or "delight." Now, in the English, the word "de-sire" is composed of two words: "de" which means *from* and "sire" which means "father." The desires in our hearts (Psalm 37) are put there from God our Father to accomplish His purpose in our lives. God delights in us (Psalm 139:13) and has given us, through new birth in Christ, the very spiritual DNA of Christ making us a part of His family (we belong) so that in every season of our lives we can live out His purpose.

When Jesus spoke to Nicodemus in John 3:3 he said, *"Verily, verily, I say unto thee, except a man be born again, he cannot see the kingdom of God."* As a believer, God has deposited a fire within your spirit giving you the indwelling new life of God. So, what do we do with the new life He gives us? It's time to get out of the old, dead season of your life, get out of the box of your ruts, routines, and lifeless busyness and start fulfilling your purpose as God's child to do good works for His glory.

Day 1 - *Get Out of Your Box*

If you are in Christ,
You are a new creation,
The old you is passing way.
Behold, every part of you is becoming new.
(2 Corinthians 5:17 paraphrased)

H e who is born of the spirit cannot live in a box, which the world and culture has invented to bury you in. The wages of sin is death. Before you are born again, you simply exist; you are part of the zombies of the walking dead...no true *LIFE* is in you. But when He, who is the Way, the Truth, and the Life, Jesus Christ comes into your existence, you are born again and begin to live for the first time since your birth. Yes, there is life after death, eternal life through Jesus Christ, but there is also life after birth in Christ when you are born again.

God holds the key to the eternal life. Do not take for granted the people, the opportunities, and the favor He has blessed you with in this season of *LIFE*. Look at what's right and not what's wrong. Thank the Lord for what you have instead of what you do not have.

See each day as a gift from God filled with purpose. You now belong to a new family, the family of God, birthed by His Spirit and living in His purpose. Tomorrow is not promised to any of us. Have you ever gone through something and felt like it was the valley of shadow of death?

During the tough times, it's easy to get discouraged. Don't give up! Press on and move forward! God is revealing His purpose and doing a good work in you as you live *LIFE* in His purpose. Remember that *"God works for the good of those who love him, who have been called according to his purpose."* (Romans 8:28 NIV).

Get out of the way and start thinking outside the box so you can see the bigger vision that is before you. Don't be complacent in your box of confinement.

Think About This...

Thank God for all the past boxes He has delivered you from. Pray with thanksgiving for the new creation you are becoming in Christ.

Learn this life lesson...say it and do it: **I am a new person in Christ Jesus—the old is passing away and I am becoming new!**

Day 2 - *Nothing to Fear*

For God has not given us a spirit of fear,
But of power and of love and of a sound mind.
(2 Timothy 1:7)

People have been running away from all the things they fear in life. But where are they running to? You can lock the door of the past with its hidden, dark sin and hurts or you can run and open the door to God's abundant joy, peace, and victory.

Why are you afraid of making decisions, confronting life's issues, and taking the risk of faith? You have nothing to fear. God's power, love, and your renewed mind in Christ will overcome every obstacle and shatter every weapon formed against you.

As a child of God, our Father lets us know there is no need to fear. God is our refuge and strength... A very present help in times of trouble. We have a greater reason to live.

When you put God first and obey His commands, you open the door for His favor and have the advantage to succeed! Even if someone has betrayed you and it looks like they are winning, you must keep reminding yourself... "I have an advantage because I am a child of God and He is in control."

God doesn't look at your failure, He looks at your faith. He shows favor to those who favor Him. Those who are favored by God know that God is with them and that nothing can happen to them apart from his good purpose. When we have favor of the Lord, we rest in confidence that our sins are forgiven, we are within the plan of God and that He is there. We also begin to see and appreciate the little blessings that God provides daily.

Because we are now alive in Christ, we celebrate life and never take His blessings for granted. For me, Life wasn't going how I thought it should. I reached a point in life where I hated God. I ran far from it all. I grew tired and empty. When I finally stopped running, there He was right where I was all along. I was blind, but now I see.

Think About This...

Alive in Christ, you have nothing to fear, nothing to hide, and nothing to lose. He protects you, forgives you, and gives you His abundant life.

Learn this life lesson...say it and do it: **I have nothing to fear, nothing to hide, nothing to lose, and everything to gain in Christ Jesus.**

Day 3 - *Becoming a New Creation*

We can't know it all. Self-made, righteous Nicodemus thought he had all the answers and the right to brag. For those that don't know, Nicodemus was a scholar and was part of a higher office Sanhedrin. While many of the Pharisees went against Jesus, Nicodemus was seeking the truth (John 3). He came to Jesus at night searching for answers to theological questions and learned he needed to be born again.

Jesus discusses one of the basic fundamental applications of doctrines of the Christian faith—newness of birth. Jesus said without new birth one cannot see the kingdom of God. It comes to those who repent of sin; turn to God, then must transition from their old life to new life of obedience to Jesus Christ. Authentic conversion and not just lip service to Christ means that one has been set free from sins and setbacks. Nicodemus in meeting face to face with Jesus received a revelation about himself. That meeting was a test of his character. Let's talk about the test that many of us are dealing with, when we see God face to face like Nicodemus did. Most of us are dealing with a test that can refine our outlook in life and build our character.

Think about This...

When you have met Jesus, describe what He revealed about your character:

_____

_____

_____

Learn this life lesson...say it and do it: **When I see myself as Jesus sees me, I must repent of the old life and be transformed by my new life in Jesus.**

Day 4 - *A Good Fight*

W e are fighting to live, fighting to be born, and are fighting to reach that height in life. I was fighting for revenge and I learned quickly, it's wasn't worth it. Nicodemus had a place of surrendering. He was longing for surrender thinking he knew it all but still was alone. You can be around people and still feel terribly isolated and alone. You can be at a gathering worshiping the Lord and still feel alone. You can be in a marriage and still feel alone. Some people have reached high places in the secular world or have played the role by putting on the mask but notice it's tiring and lonely at the top. You are asking God, *when can I be real with my*self?

We learn in Matthew 16:26 that there is no benefit in gaining all the world has to offer if we lose our soul in the process. What are you exchanging in this life for your soul? Is anything in this world worth losing one's soul?

Why gain it all and still feel empty, alone, and in despair? Nicodemus came to a place when he needed to hear what God was saying. There will be a point in each person's life when the opportunity presents itself to come to God. Only He can give you a life of hope, born with a purpose, born of the Spirit of God, like a baby in the womb about to be born.

When you are Born Again, God will finish the good work He has started in you. He fights with you through every circumstance in life. Any fight or struggle you now find yourself in as a Christian is an opportunity right now for your breakthrough. You may feel like the child in the Bible that is are dying and without breath. Not true! The breath of God's Spirit from you being born again is in you. The Holy Spirit will revive you, give you strength to fight through your trials, and be victorious. I went into a fight secure because I had friends that were going to fight with me but that number quickly dwindled and in the end I found myself alone. I am so thankful that now I don't have to fight my battles because now God fights them for me. I just need to trust Him.

Think About This...

1 Timothy 6:12 tells us to *"Fight the good fight of the faith. Take hold of the eternal life to which you were called when you made your good confession in the presence of many witnesses."* (NIV). What fight are you fighting?

Learn this lesson...Say it and do it: **I will not trust in my own strength and ability. I will forgive and I will surrender to God and trust Him to fight my battles. Victory is mine in Jesus name.**

Day 5 - *Life with His Purpose*

Today I am living in that full purpose that God had destined for me even before I was in my mother's womb. It's crazy how you can't see the fullness of God when you are in darkness but when you allow yourself to be in the light and completely free, you feel God's light shining through you.

Sometimes people think that the years we are in darkness before being saved, or even in the trials we go through as Christians are lost and wasted time. I'm here to tell you that every season God has purposed us to go through, refines and shapes our character to be more like His. Read (Romans 5) again and rejoice in all the victories you have experienced in Christ.

At the End of This Week...

Take a couple of days and write down a few things you have learned this week:

- *About Yourself...*
- *About God...*
- *About one way you need to change...*

Week 6 -
A Name Change

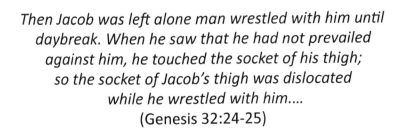

*Then Jacob was left alone man wrestled with him until
daybreak. When he saw that he had not prevailed
against him, he touched the socket of his thigh;
so the socket of Jacob's thigh was dislocated
while he wrestled with him....*
(Genesis 32:24-25)

*God, furthermore, said to Moses, "Thus you shall say
to the sons of Israel, The LORD, the God of your fathers,
the God of Abraham, the God of Isaac, and the God of
Jacob, has sent me to you.' This is My name forever, and
this is My memorial-name to all generations. Go and
gather the elders of Israel together and say to them,
'The LORD, the God of your fathers, the God of Abraham,
Isaac and Jacob, has appeared to me, saying,
I am indeed concerned about you and what
has been done to you in Egypt....'"*
(Exodus 3:15)

God made a covenant with Abraham, Isaac, and Jacob which was a pact with human kind. Abraham was a man of faith. God promised Abraham that he would make him a great nation. He was a man who feared God, obeyed God, and was tested. In all that he did, Abraham accepted God's will for him.

Isaac was a man of prayer, a man that made altars and offering unto the Lord. On the other hand, Jacob seemed to be the odd one out in this trio but God loved Jacob in spite of his faults.

Day 1 - *God Loves Imperfect People*

Jacob was a shady person, a trickster, a good lair, supplanter, and deceiver. He was person who only thought of himself. How many of us know someone like that, it's only about them? How can they benefit from you? If you think about it and we could write down names for days.

Have you even thought maybe you could relate to Jacob's character? The way he acted, why he always tried to take advantage of people. Jacob was a manipulator. He tried to get people to do what he wanted not what God wanted.

Perhaps, Jacob picked up many of his bad habits from his mother Rebecca. Doesn't make sense when the Lord can see all your mistakes, does it? We can live life with destiny in our own hands, but during that whole time, Jesus will have His hand on us. In spite of what we want, we can only run away from him for so long. We can play the blame game, but for how long. How much longer are we going to run from God? With all of his wheeling and dealing, Jacob didn't measure up to the legacy he had received from Abraham and Isaac.

Jacob had bad habits in his life just like I did...just like all of us. At some point in our lives, we have to stop fooling and blaming others for the bad things that happened to us. Remember, God loves us too much to fail us. God wants the best for us yet we refuse His best. Are you ready

JACOB LOPEZ

for God to take control of your destiny? Are you ready to surrender to God's plan for your life?

Think About This...

Jacob's name spoke of his natural destiny as a trickster and a sup planter. But that wasn't God's destiny for him. Jacob needed a life change and it would start with a name change.

Learn this life lesson...say it and do it: **I need to give up my own defined destiny. I need God's good plans for my life.**

Day 2 - *Stop Running from God*

J acob ended up running from his family, his place in the family, and God's plan for his life. But God spoke a word over Jacob's life, and today as you read this book, God is speaking a word over you.

No more running, it's time to surrender your sorrow,
your pain, your darkest secrets.
Even if you don't want to go to church,
I am still your God.
Even if you have given up on life, I am still your God.
Even if you still dealing with a broken marriage,
I am still your God.
You have been for years trying to give CPR
to your dead dreams,
but I am still your God.
I was your God when you left church.
I was your God when you were backsliding.
I was your God when everyone turned their back on you.
I was your God when you were about to commit suicide.

Jacob ran away from everyone he knew; he was completely alone in life like Moses, Jeremiah, Daniel, and Paul. Jacob was running from his brother Esau, because Esau was furious and vowed to kill him for manipulating him and taking his birthright.

Truth is you have the option of running and running and find yourself in the same place you started running from or stop running and start resting in God's plan for your life. You have the option to live in peace with yourself, others and more importantly God or live a life full of accomplishments and success and yet feel completely alone.

This is your season! This is the day the Lord has made! Today is the day you stop running and you start trusting. You stop living in the shadows and walk in the fullness of God's light for your life. Today is the day you not only look well put together on the outside but you're also put together on the inside. Today is the day you confront your past and declare you will no longer keep looking back but you will keep your eyes on Jesus.

Think About This...

Do you feel lonely, abandoned, forsaken and forgotten? God to never leave or forsake you. So, why are you running away?

Learn this life lesson...say it and do it: **I will stop running away from God and start running toward Him!**

Day 3 - *Wrestling with God*

W e read the story of Jacob as he wrestled with the Angel of the Lord, Jacob's thigh was dislocated and he had to yield. Sometimes the Lord has to humble us, and that can be a hard place for you to be in. God will always win the wrestling match. Maybe if Jacob was wiser, he would have submitted sooner. But, we are as hardheaded as Jacob was. We think we can wrestle and manipulate God just like we do with people.

If we can learn something from Jacob, we can discover that when we wrestle against God there will be nothing but opposition. Fleeing from his family had been bad enough, but then wrestling with God took Jacob on a journey he never could have imagined. Jacob the deceiver received a new name, *Israel*. His destiny wasn't defined by his past, his family, or his running. His destiny was defined by God's future for him and for the nation that would come out of his twelve sons—the Nation of Israel.

Think About This…

You may have let your family, your past, your mistakes, or your running away define you. You may have been called names by others, but now God has a new name for you and your future. Are you tired of wrestling with God and your past? Are you ready for a new name, a new hope, a new future with God?

Learn this life lesson…say it and do it: **I am named and defined by God—no one or nothing else!**

Day 4 - *Ready to Change?*

O nce you are broken and beaten, you will understand who you are fighting with. In life, our biggest enemy is ourselves. Who do you see in the mirror every day? The greatest enemy you will ever fight. Spiritually speaking, God has to change your name and your identity. Most of us have been identified with an old name others have given to us. It's time for a change.

The Lord promises in the book of Revelation to give us a new name. Jesus says that to him or her who overcomes, He will give a new name (Revelation 3:12). Let the old name be your Cross. Crucify the old name, the old self, and let God rename you anew. If any person is in Christ, that person is a new creation. Jacob, the old you, needs to die. Israel, the new you, needs to be born.

Paul wrote about it this way, *"I have been crucified with Christ; it is no longer I who live, but Christ lives in me; and the life which I now live in the flesh I live by faith in the Son of God, who loved me and gave Himself for me"* (Galatians 2:20-21). Let Jacob be your Cross and Israel be your destiny. The old you is dying but the new you is a new creation, a new identity in Christ Jesus.

Think About This...

Change begins with you! Decide to stop running from the call God has upon your life. Decide to walk into your destiny and purpose.

Learn this life lesson...say it and do it: **I am ready now to live with my new name in Christ Jesus.**

Day 5 - *What Is Your Limp?*

S ometimes you will wake up as Jacob or Israel the choice is yours. The battle is daily but the question reminds, who will win? God wants you to yield. He wants to give you a new name. "And he said, *'Your name shall no longer be Jacob, but Israel; for you have striven with God and with men and have prevailed.'* (Genesis 32:28) Israel means, "He who strives with God."

He was no longer a Jacob; he was now Israel. Jacob fought with God and lost. Jacob had to give up. Are you willing to give it all up for Jesus? The place where God will turn your sorrows into joy, the place where God will call you His son or daughter, the place where God can heal you from your past, the place where you are ready to open your heart, the place where God will forgive you, and make everything new.

Jacob's limp is a great reminder of his humbling wrestling experience with God. What if we look deeper inside ourselves and find Jacob is still there? It will always be a high price to pay. Do you dare to become Israel? Do you dare to speak life into Jacob?

The question remains for those who might try this: *how badly do you want your name change?*

Oftentimes God uses the hurt in our lives to bring us back to a place of surrender. God's love is to put us in the proper place, so that we can cling only to Him. Our weakness will be a sign that we can't win without Jesus.

Jacob knew about God, but didn't know God. He was fighting with his identity. He was wrestling for his Cross to obtain his destiny. God changed Jacob to Israel right in the book of Genesis but in the book of Exodus 3:15-16, *"The LORD, the God of your fathers, the God of Abraham, Isaac and Jacob."* God had both renamed Jacob and also validated him as a patriarch of Israel. God could have said, "I am the God of Abraham, Isaac and Israel."

Take a moment and think how amazing our Lord is. He's there when we mess up, give up, or walk away. God doesn't and won't give up on us. He didn't give up on Jacob. For years, I was running away from God. He found me and saved me in the midst of being shot and left dying on the street. You can stop running. God can redeem your past and give you a new name, a new future in Christ. Will you stop running away and wrestling with God?

At the End of This Week...

Take a couple of days and write down a few things you have learned this week:

- *About Yourself...*
- *About God...*
- *About one way you need to change...*

Week 7 -

The Forgotten

The hand of the LORD was upon me, and carried me out
in the spirit of the LORD, and set me down
in the midst of the valley which was full of bones,
And caused me to pass by them round about: and,
behold, there were very many in the open valley;
and, lo, they were very dry.
And he said unto me, Son of man, can these bones live?
And I answered, O Lord GOD, thou knowest....
(Ezekiel 37:1-3)

God answers Ezekiel's question in verse 9. He tells Ezekiel to speak to those dry bones that they may live...come to life!

You may feel forgotten by God just like the bones in Ezekiel's vision. But a simple word from God breathed life into those dry bones. They stood up like an army. What was dead, came alive. The nation was restored physically and spiritually.

Dry bones are a picture of the Jews in captivity, scattered, and dead as a nation, as a people. Nothing is impossible with God. A valley of dry bones can live.

Day 1 - *Are You a Valley of Dry Bones?*

P erhaps you feel dead like that valley of dry bones. Maybe you lost something along the way. Maybe some of us were in a dry place in our life or still in a dry place with no hope, no voice, or no peace. Maybe it was friends or even family. Maybe you loved someone and the relationship dried up. Something else got your attention. Sometimes we give CPR to something that is dead. Your marriage is in a dry place, a dead place. Your kids don't even know you anymore. The passion you had just went dry. How can we change that?

God is calling a Generation of Ezekiel's to speak life to the generations present and to come. It's time for us to speak life to fathers, mothers, and our children. We must speak God's life even when people have lost hope in their communities, neighborhoods, and the world. God will bring life to spiritually dead dreams. God will restore your marriage. God will bring back what the devil thought he took from you. He will bring that son or daughter that you lost relationship with. I believe He will and can, can you believe?

Say to yourself, *God won't forget me.*

Think About This...

Even if I feel like a heap of old, dry bones, God feels differently about me. He sees me a worth being restored, revived, and resurrected. He can take anything that is dry in my life and bring it to life.

Learn this life lesson...say it and do it: **God hasn't forgotten me. He is restoring, renewing, and giving me new life.**

Day 2 - *Speak Life not Death*

Proverbs 18:21 reminds us that *life and death are in the power of the tongue.* The breath of God is in you. The Holy Spirit dwells in you and can speak through you. You can breathe life or death into your future. God has not forgotten you.

Say it like you mean it that God will remember you. Speak life to yourself and what's around you. You don't have to be at the same location to speak life into it. The hand of the Lord was upon me (I am chosen) in the middle of the graveyard filled with bullets. He did not forget me. He hasn't forgotten you.

God is waiting for Israel, for you, for your family, for your future generations to have the fresh breath of His Spirit breathed upon them and give them life. Speak life not death to yourself and all future generations.

Think About This...

Who is God wanting you to speak life into besides yourself...a spouse? A parent? A child? A relative? Another friend? Another Christian or Christian leader? Make a list. Start speaking life not death into yourself and others.

Learn this life lesson...say it and do it: **I will speak life not death to myself and everyone around me.**

Day 3 - *Don't Tolerate Death*

Are you willing to stand in the middle of life and death for those that have been dead because no one has spoken words of hope? We see dry bones dead for a long time. When people don't change, or even know how too, no one was there to come alongside them. When are we not going to think about ourselves and think about others? How many people we know in our families that were forgotten.

- Great man or woman of God
- Great ministers
- Great gifted and talented family
- Great fathers
- Great mothers
- Great coaches
- Great mentors
- _____(Add to this list.)

Think About This...

Take time to remember some of the forgotten people in your family's past who need your prayers and possibly you to reach out to them personally with God's love, mercy, and grace. Pray. Make a list and obey God.

Learn this life lesson...say it and do it: **God has not forgotten me. I will not forget others. I will pray and reach out with God's love as God has reached out to me.**

Day 4 - *Stand in the Gap for Others...Don't Give Up on Them*

Many of us have given up on people knowing we knew we could have helped. There was no one to stand in the graveyard and speak life, and pray for them. Ezekiel saw bones, but God saw an army. Get a vision for what God sees, for the potential in others, instead of their dead bones of mistakes, failures, and past sins.

In Ezekiel 22:30, God is looking for someone to stand in the gap for His people—to pray and intercede for them. God's people had wandered away from faithfully serving the Living God to worshipping idols. Nonetheless, God did not give up on them or forget them. Regardless of how family members or friends have hurt you or abandoned God, we cannot give up on them. We can stand in the gap and pray for them—for their salvation, healing, restoration, deliverance, and renewal. While they may appear to be dead spiritually, God sees life.

When will you see life and not death in others? Are you willing to pray for them and stand in the gap? God hasn't forgotten them or given up on them?

Think About This...

In what way can you stand in the gap for others? At this very moment, who do you know among family, friends, and colleagues needing prayer, help, support, affirmation, or hope from you?

Learn this life lesson...say it and do it: **I will listen to God and stand in the gap for those who need him.**

Day 5 - *Start Over Again*

Perhaps it is now time for your second wind, your time to start over again. Even if you have been forgotten, God has not forgotten you. The forgotten are many but can these bones rise again? God has not forgotten your dreams, your purpose, your destiny, your family, your calling over your life. God is about to transport you to speak life to those areas in your life that kept you out of the will of God.

We read in Exodus 2:24, that God did not forget the Israelites when they were in bondage in Egypt. "*So God heard their groaning; and God remembered His covenant with Abraham, Isaac, and Jacob.*" Likewise, the Scriptures remind us in Genesis 8:1, "*But God remembered Noah and all the wild animals and the livestock that were with him in the ark, and he sent a wind over the earth, and the waters receded.*" Yes, God does remember Noah, and God extends mercy to all mankind, of whom God would not fully destroy. He is the God of second chances.

But let's also view it another way. Many of us today can lose it all; in those times, God may be so silent that we may never understand *why* certain bad things happen to us. What do we do in that case; how do we handle it? Noah asked God for mercy, but what do you do when you do not see God's mercy for months or years. Look at how long Noah had to work hard, build an ark, and wait on God's mercy. God is patient with you; are you willing to be patient with Him? Will you continue to pray no matter how long it takes? You may feel alone in those dark seasons when it seemed that God and others forgot you and walked away from you. You loved people, they didn't love you back.

Will you persevere and trust God no matter how long it takes?

At the End of This Week...

Take a couple of days and write down a few things you have learned this week:

- *About Yourself...*
- *About God...*
- *About one way you need to change...*

Week 8 -

Time to Decide

Shadrach, Meshach and Abed-nego replied to the king, "O Nebuchadnezzar, we do not need to give you an answer concerning this matter. "If it be so, our God whom we serve is able to deliver us from the furnace of blazing fire; and He will deliver us out of your hand, O king. But even if He does not, let it be known to you, O king, that we are not going to serve your gods or worship the golden image that you have set up."
(Daniel 3:16-18)

The time came in my life when I had to finally stop trying to please others or myself and start pleasing God. Pleasing anything or anyone else other than God means that I am bowing down to idols. Idolatry is forbidden in the Ten Commandments. As Christians, we rarely see ourselves as being idolatrous; we judge people in other religions as being idol worshippers. The truth is that anyone or thing we exalt above Christ at any time in our lives is idolatry. Examine yourself in every decision you make: *are you serving Christ alone or an idol?*

Day 1 - *Be Bold in Pleasing God not Man*

Daniel and his friends made a decision for God instead of seeking to please man. They decided to do the right thing...together. However, in your personal walk with the Lord, there may be times when your friends will not choose to walk with you through a fiery test of faithfulness to God. They may ask you why they should walk with you and grill you with such questions as...

- Are you smart enough or talented enough to do what's, right?
- Will you be able to stand up to persecution or criticism?
- After we step into the fire, what will happen next?
- What will others think about us? Will our friends or family members reject us?

Think About This...

Read over the questions above. Have you been asking yourself any of these lately? If so, how are you answering them?

Learn this life lesson...say it and do it: **I choose to be unashamed, bold, and courageous in following Christ.**

Day 2 - *Some May Not Be Able to Follow Christ with You*

Y ou have read my story. I have had to make some tough decisions in following Christ which caused me to lose relationships with those whom I thought were with me... but they couldn't go on the journey with me.

I could not make my decisions in following Christ based on how I thought others would accept or reject me. Scripture tells us that we *ought to walk out our faith in a way that pleases God and not men* (1 Thessalonians 4; Hebrews 11). Daniel and his friends were bold, fearless, and courageous in deciding to follow God. Joshua made the same kind of fearless decision centuries before when he stood before Israel and said,

Serve the Lord!
And if it seems evil to you to serve the Lord,
choose for yourselves this day whom you will serve,
whether the gods which your fathers served that were
on the other side of the River,
or the gods of the Amorites,
in whose land you dwell. But as for me and my house,
we will serve the Lord.
(Joshua 24:14-15)

Think About This…

This choice isn't just a one-time choice…it's daily. The enemy will tempt you daily to choose between God's way and the wrong way, your way, or the way of pleasing others. Don't be caught napping; when you least expect it you will be tempted to do the wrong thing.

Learn this life lesson…say it and do it: **I choose TODAY to serve the Lord.**

Day 3 - *Christ Is Your First Love*

Y ou cannot base your decisions on what others will think or if they will go with you. Christ must be your first priority, your first love. When others hesitate, criticize, or urge you to turn away from the Lord, don't let their fear, uncertainty, or doubts dissuade you. *"Do not be afraid of them, for I am with you and will rescue you," declares the LORD"* (Jeremiah 1:8).

One of the primary tactics the enemy uses is shame to distract you from choosing what is right. Someone may say to you, "You should be ashamed of the way you are treating _____ by being a religious zealot or legalist." Shaming you can take on all kinds of words or forms, but the bottom line is that when you turn away from doing what's right, you are ashamed of the Gospel of Jesus Christ. Paul writes in Romans 1, *"For I am not ashamed of the gospel of Jesus Christ, for it is the power of God to salvation for everyone who believes..."* (Romans 1:9).

Think About This...

Is someone or some organization trying to shame you into doing things the wrong way instead of obeying God's ways? How will you resist the temptation of pleasing others instead of God?

Learn this life lesson...say it and do it: **My first and only priority today is loving and serving Jesus Christ.**

Day 4 - *Decide to Turn Away from the Old and Embrace God's New*

You have heard the cliché, "Not to decide is to decide." I had to decide to leave my old thoughts, old ways, old friends, and old behaviors. As a new person in Jesus Christ, I had to go through the fiery cleansing of God's Spirit as the old was passing away and all things were becoming new in my life. Daniel's friends faced a fiery furnace; you and I may have to face some fire as well as the stinging works and burning criticism of some of those closest to us are trying to turn us away from following Christ. Are you willing to be like one of Daniel's friends? Will you go through the fire no matter the cost? Will you surrender all?

Shadrach, Meshach and Abed-nego made a powerful point. They told King Nebuchadnezzar that even if God didn't spare them from the fire, they would still not bow down to idols. Too often we try to bargain with God when He tells us to do what's right and we want the promise of a reward before we act. We say something like, "God, if you do so and so, then I will follow you." Let's be Christ followers because we love Him and because we love Him, we obey Him.

Think About This…

Are you willing to obey Christ even if there is no reward? Are you willing to obey Christ and surrender it all to Him? To move forward with the kind of Spirit-imparted courage that Daniel's friends had, I invite you to say and memorize the statements below:

Learn these life lesson...say it and do it:

- **I am not going to allow anyone to dictate my destiny.**
- **I am not going to allow anyone to speak negativity into my life.**
- **I am not going to allow others or circumstances to determine my faith.**
- **I am not going to allow people distract me.**
- **I must obey God rather than what others tell me to believe.**

Day 5 - *Be Bold*

D aniel's friends exemplified the courage and boldness that Joshua Chapter 1 speaks of:

Only be strong and very courageous, that you may
observe to do according to all the law which Moses
My servant commanded you; do not turn from
it to the right hand or to the left,
that you may prosper wherever you go.
This Book of the Law shall not depart from your mouth,
but you shall meditate in it day and night, that you may
observe to do according to all that is written in it.
For then you will make your way prosperous, and then
you will have good success.
Have I not commanded you?
Be strong and of good courage;
do not be afraid, nor be dismayed,
for the Lord your God is with you wherever you go.
(Joshua 1:7-9 emphasis added)

What attributes did Daniel's friend exhibited that you need to ask God to deepen and strengthen in your own faith? Check them off and then pray fervently:

- € Courage
- € Faith
- € Boldness

- € Passion
- € First love for Christ
- € Fearlessness
- € Hope
- € Confidence
- € _____

At the End of This Week...

Take a couple of days and write down a few things you have learned this week:

- *About Yourself...*
- *About God...*
- *About one way you need to change...*

Week 9 -

Why Does God Allow Difficulties in Our Lives?

A t times, God allows trials to take place because He is trying to accomplish His purposes in our lives. God is not the author of confusion; however, He will allow us to go through things that test our faith and build our character. Often, we bring problems into our own lives due to disobedience or neglecting our relationship with God.

It's always easier to complain than to trust God perfect plan in our lives. The truth is bad things happen to good people and good things happen to bad people but there is a day of judgement. Don't get so caught up on the fact that you're facing hard times and trials. Don't get caught up asking "Why me? "

One day we will all stand before the Lord and we will be judged according to our actions here on earth. Let us live today to the best of our ability. Let us live a life that is pleasing and honoring to God. Let us live a life that forgives and forgets. Let us live a life that loves even if we get hurt in the process. Let us live our life following the Cross of Jesus.

Day 1 - *A Rough Life*

W hen we are in the middle of a trial, we must stand on the Word and recognize that if it doesn't kill us, it will make us better. Consider these reflections.

A rough life:
caught up in a web of lies in the hood
   with gangs feeling high,
      feeling good, looking good,
         walking in style trying to fill every void
         in my heart.
            if I would confess my truths: where
            would I start?

Raised and born in the gospel,
   yet looking for something more earthly pleasures,
      didn't know what was in store
         I thought I had it all together with
         everything I wanted
            then I hit rock bottom:

I wouldn't even flaunt it shot seven times!
   Laid for dead and nowhere to run
      I thought I would be confronted with a gun,
         I had it all together, I thought, but...
            this is NOT how it was suppose to be.

I was at the wrong place and with bad company.
My life was passing by, not knowing what to do.
Suddenly I heard my mother's voice, "I'm with you....
Call out the name of Jesus for there is power
in His name.
It's a matter of life and death with no time for games.
With everything I had in me, I called unto the Lord.

Next thing I knew, I was restored.
Here I am to testify of God's mercy upon my life.
I don't even deserve it, but he gave me a chance
to fight,
to continue on my journey but NOT without Him.

As I continue to share my story,
there's one ultimate truth for you to know:
only with Jesus you can be completely free.

Think About This...

No matter what imprisons you, or what chains from the past hold you captive, Jesus is the One who sets captives free. He will set you free! Run to Him. What wrong thoughts, feelings, and behaviors do you need to be set free from right now?

Learn this life lesson...say it and do it: **Jesus sets the captives free. The truth Jesus reveals to me is setting me free.**

Day 2 - *Humble Yourself*

And you shall remember that the Lord your God led you all the way these forty years in the wilderness, to humble you and test you, to know what was in your heart, whether you would keep His commandments or not. So He humbled you, allowed you to hunger, and fed you with manna which you did not know nor did your fathers know, that He might make you know that man shall not live by bread alone; but man lives by every word that proceeds from the mouth of the Lord.
(Deuteronomy 8:2-3)

God alone is God. In our wilderness trials, He is able to fulfill His will in us by allowing certain trials to take place that will break down our pride and humble us. A humble person is one who will obey God.

God humbles you so that you will submit to His Word and His way of doing things. Trials help you develop perseverance, patience, and character. Humility reveals your heart and passion for God as your source for everything in life.

God has the authority to cause storms to get you to acknowledge Him and run to Him. Memorize these important words:

"Therefore humble yourselves under the mighty hand of God, that He may exalt you in due time, casting all your care upon Him, for He cares for you" (1 Peter 5:6-7).

Think About This...

Identify the areas of selfish pride in your life and relationships that need to be confessed. Repent and allow God to humble you.

Learn this life lesson...say it and do it: **Lord Jesus Christ, humble me, forgive me, grant me Your mercy.**

Day 3 - *Be Grateful*

For He commands and raises the stormy wind,
Which lifts up the waves of the sea.
(Psalm 107:25)

Through the storms in life, God will show you why you should be grateful: *because he is loving.* In the most difficult trials of my life, I realized that it was God who got me through. In His mercy, I survived, got stronger, and started running with God instead of from Him.

Sometimes, going through pain will help you understand something about yourself that you didn't know before. (Psalm 119: 71). Think about, you will never know who you are until hard moments come. God will allow the consequences of slackness and disobedience to take their course your life. Every commandment God gives carries with it judgment, if it is disobeyed. When you have to experience negative consequences from your actions, God's love kicks in to try to get you to stop going in the wrong direction and change your course.

We deal with so many reasons that God allows trials in our lives. He loves you. God knows that disobedience will cause you to be trapped in sin, so He will allow a trial to come to keep you from being caught in a trap. God can cause things to get so uncomfortable for you when you disobey Him, that you will have no choice but to change directions. In everything, give thanks for His changes and new opportunities.

Think About This...

Feeling uncomfortable? God allows you to be uncomfortable so you will seek His guidance and comfort instead of trying to create your own comfortable answers and solutions to your dilemmas.

Learn this life lesson...say it and do it: **I take responsibility for my decisions and their consequences so that I may learn from God how to change for the better.**

Day 4 - *Starts and Stops*

He will cause spiritual stoppers to guide you into the right place. Winston Nunes once said that God leads by starts and stops. In other words, He wants your attention. We may allow our attention to be taken away from God and given to other things. We can be so busy doing the work of the ministry that we can't hear God telling us how to be effective in ministry. He can't trust us with the big things until we learn to take care of the small thing. He wants to remove every hindrance in your fellowship with Him.

God wants to remove every hindrance that keeps you from being fully yielded to Him. Have you made someone or something your idol? He wants us to love him. If God has to allow trials in our lives it's so that we can love and acknowledge Him more.

Let's take it deeper and be real with ourselves. Examine yourself. Ask your heart, "Am I passionately in love with Christ Jesus? Is my life fulfilling the two great commandments of totally loving God, and loving others like myself? If you are in love with God, then the things you need will show up. God knows how to get you to spend time with Him. Some of us haven't hit rock bottom yet. Judge yourself every day, so you won't be judged. The love of God will always be working on your behalf; even in the middle of a hard time. Thank God in everything; give Him praise no matter what you're going through.

Let's remember Jesus also had a "rough experience. *"The Spirit immediately drove him [Jesus] out into the wilderness. And he was in the wilderness forty days, being tempted by Satan. And he was with the wild animals, and the angels were ministering to him"* (Mark 1:12-13).

Note that it was the Spirit of God that pushed Jesus into the wilderness temptation. If Jesus had it hard, do you think you will have it easy. *NOT!* He went through the wilderness just as Israel did centuries before. Submit yourself to the wilderness experiences that God leads you through. The operative word here is "through." Trust God to lead you through wildernesses, trials, temptations, and the valleys of the shadow of death (Psalm 23).

Think About This...

Are you in a wilderness right now? If so, don't fight God or blame others for your temptations. Get intimate with God...so close that you can feel His breath and hear the whisper of His voice. Trust Him totally to walk you through.

Learn this life lesson...say it and do it: **God is leading me through my wilderness and into His promises.**

Day 5 - *Seize Opportunities from God*

W e don't need to "miss our moments" we need to "make our moments." When God's opportunities present themselves, we need to seize the moment and grab ahold of God and all that He has for us. We are co-creators of the events with God. Many of the events in our lives seem to be "outside of our control," and yet, because we tend to do things unconsciously, we fail to realize that we have at some level created the events by our beliefs, behaviors, and language. Our hard times will make us and build us because Jesus is always creating something – we need to create consciously and lead consciously. Let's not get in God's way.

The worldview in which you think, feel, and act is the world as you choose to perceive it. It is the same for the people around you. If your people are to change, it is essential that the first thing that changes is the way they view their world (worldview), the way they view themselves, and the way they view their situations. See the world from God's perspective. Ditch every other worldview. Remember what God says to you continually:

"Forget the former things;
do not dwell on the past.
See, I am doing a new thing!
Now it springs up; **do you not perceive it?**
I am making a way in the desert

and streams in the wasteland."
(Isaiah 43:18-19 NIV emphasis added)

At the End of This Week...

Take a couple of days and write down a few things you have learned this week:

- *About Yourself...*
- *About God...*
- *About one way you need to change...*

Week 10 -

Pain Pushes You to Your Destiny

*Then Jonah prayed unto the LORD HIS GOD
OUT OF THE FISH'S BELLY,
AND SAID, I CRIED BY REASON OF MINE AFFLICTION
UNTO THE LORD, AND HE HEARD ME;
OUT OF THE BELLY OF HELL CRIED I,
AND THOU HEARDEST MY VOICE.
FOR THOU HADST CAST ME INTO THE DEEP,
IN THE MIDST OF THE SEAS;
AND THE FLOODS COMPASSED ME ABOUT:
ALL THY BILLOWS AND THY WAVES PASSED OVER ME.*
(Jonah 2:1-3 KJV)

Author Henry Clouds asserts, "We change our behavior when the pain of staying the same becomes greater than the pain of changing. Consequences give us the pain that motivates us to change."[2] Jonah was running from God. You know my story; like Jonah, I was running from God. In great pain, Jonah finally reached out to God.

Often when we are running from God and praying for God to deliver us from the consequences and pain of our rebellion, we pray for God to change our circumstances. We should be asking God to change us. Things had to get so bad for Jonah that he finally turned to God for help instead of running away. The consequences of his rebellion hurt so badly, that he was willing to repent and change.

Remember that Jonah was called to take the news of God's mercy to the unsaved. Likewise, God is always speaking to us to reach the unsaved. At times, we think of only what we can gain knowing it's not about us. God told Jonah *"Arise, go to Nineveh, that great city, and cry against it, for their wickedness is come up before me"*. Sometimes God will take you back to, the place that almost killed you, a place where you failed, a place where everyone turned on you.

Now that my life has change for the best, I find myself going back where I almost lost my life. This time not to fight but to preach the Gospel to those that hurt me at one time in my journey.

When you think, you can run from God, think again. You can't run from God. Remember the words of Psalm 139:

Where can I go from Your Spirit?
Or where can I flee from Your presence?
If I ascend into heaven, you are there;
If I make my bed in hell, behold, you are there.
If I take the wings of the morning,
And dwell in the uttermost parts of the sea,
Even there Your hand shall lead me,
And Your right hand shall hold me.
If I say, "Surely the darkness shall fall on me,"
Even the night shall be light about me;
Indeed, the darkness shall not hide from You,
But the night shines as the day;
The darkness and the light are both alike to You.
(Psalm 139:7-12)

You think you can? Let's try to break this down, maybe our life events can tie into Jonah. The Lord sent out a great wind into the sea. The Lord prepared a great fish to swallow him. Check this out: how many times has God called us and then sent great trials our way? When the difficulties arose, when our fears threw cold water on our lukewarm faith, we ran. Then the merciful Lord spoke the second time and the pain from our earlier disobedience finally helped us turn from our self-centered ways and toward God.

When we are born in pain, we die in pain. Much of that pain is of our own creation. When we sleep, we sleep in pain, we wake up in pain. When we sing, we sing in pain? We worship, we worship in pain. When we talk to our kids, we talk in pain. When we go to work, we go in pain. I feel pain because I go to church. You feel pain even when you leave church. When I feel joy, I feel pain. Everything that I do is in pain. I even got saved because I was in pain. Everything around my life is on pain. We always think the Lord will call us when we are at our best. Often, its at the lowest points in life, God calls us, asking us to do the impossible. Has that ever happened to you?

Day 1 - *Are You Running from God?*

P ut your name into Jonah's story. What is God calling you to do that you have run from? Could it be that some of the pain you are feeling now is the consequence of your running from God?

The Lord will send a fish or whatever is needed to get your attention. God will use the bad but use it for good.

God sent a fish to swallow Jonah; look at how powerful it was to swallow him alive. The question is what was going inside the fish (whale) with Jonah. Perhaps Jonah feared for his life in going to the enemy's capital and preaching about God's judgment. People often killed the messenger who bears the truth of bad news instead of learning from the message brought to them. Remember that running from God has consequences. When we face difficult situations which arise as consequences from our sins, will we repent or continue to blame God or others for our self-inflicted difficulties?

Think About This...

God has given you the Good News of Christ to share with family, gang members, the lost, the enemies of your life, and even with those at work. What will you do? Run away or obey?

Learn this life lesson...say it and do it: **I choose to obey God instead of running away.**

Day 2 - *Alpha and Omega*

In Revelation 22:13 Jesus tells us, *"I am the Alpha and the Omega, the First and the Last, the Beginning and the End."* What God can't do in our lives because of our resistance in Alpha, He will do it in Omega. It's the process between Alpha and Omega where God breaks us and builds us. Remember that the broken bone when it mends is always stronger. In breaking us, God removes the darkness in our minds and hearts and shines through lighting our way with His truth, guidance, and direction.

Nineveh could be your family, classmates, church members, colleagues at work, neighbors, friends, or even yourself. God is waiting for us to rise above our problems, over our mindset, over our past, and over our pain. God is calling us to be destiny changers or people who change destiny like Abraham, Noah, Moses, Deborah, Esther, David, Mary, Hannah, Priscilla, Aquilla, or Paul. God is looking down from heaven for someone to pick up the mantel that was left in the Garden of Eden due to Adam and Eve's rebellion.

Stop resisting, running, or rebelling. Allow God to change you so He doesn't have to break you. Change may be painful for a time but it's short-term pain for a long-term gain. Will you allow God to change you in the process between Alpha and Omega?

Think About This...

Running only increases your pain. Resistance only makes life harder. Repentance and change allows for the short-term pain to be transformed into long-term gain.

Learn this life lesson...say it and do it: **I will repent, change, and be transformed into Christ's image.**

Day 3 - *Passing God's Test*

Let's look at the life of King David. David killed the lion, then the bear, and then the giant. We always think it was the devil. No it was the plan of God. The trials the Lord allows us to go through are certain indicators that He is taking us higher. The Lord will test us and see if we will pass the test. We need to thank God for low levels, wide levels, and deeper levels He walks us through to reach the higher levels. That's the will of our Father.

Jonah was in God's process inside that fish. David's was in God's process in fighting the lion, bear, and giant. Peter was in God's process in the courtyard as he was denying His Lord three times. Jesus was in God's process on the Cross. Was He? Could it be He took up part of my process? The part that I could not carry successfully? The part that required me to die the death of the Cross? Are you willing to stay in God's process so that He can conform you to the image of His Son? (Read Philippians 2).

Think About This...

Becoming like Jesus is a process of being humbled, becoming a servant, and letting him lift you up. Get off your pedestal. Stop trying to be your own savior. Cry out for help from the Savior—Jesus.

Learn this life lesson...say it and do it: **I will stay in God's process until I am conformed to the image of Jesus Christ.**

Day 4 - *Jesus Set Me Free*

L et's think for one moment, *what was the issue with Jonah and us to force us to hear God's message of hope.* The Gospel club is not based on what we do but what God has done for us. We need to learn to present ourselves to the Lord in prayer instead of running away from God asking God to bless us in our running instead of putting us into a process of repentance.

What can learn from pain which pushes us toward our destiny? How does affliction open us up to hearing from God? How can we connect with Jonah who chose to run instead of obey?

A journey of uncertainty and chaos,
    Living without thought,
        A purposeless life filled with destruction,
            Yet seeming to be fun with games, women,
            drugs, and gangs.
Fame or notoriety I had,
    Loved by family and friends,
        But not ever imagining what might happen
        in the end.
I was cool, young, and reckless,
    Until one, cold night the unexpected happened.
        Shot by a gang member and left for dead.
In the end, I heard my mother's voice call on the name of Jesus,
    To rescue and save me,

To set me free.
With fear and dread,
 I called on the name of Jesus.
 He heard and helped me,
  Jesus set me free.

Think About This...

God is the God of the second chances. I had mine. You can have yours. Here is my prayer for you just as my mother prayed for me. I pray you call upon the name of Jesus. He will set you free.

Learn this life lesson...say it and do it: **Jesus help me, save me, set me free.**

Day 5 - *Listen to the Right Voice*

Mom's prayer was the right thing for me. I heard her voice and made a right choice. Now I can testify of His goodness, grace and love and each day I thank the Lord for another day from above.

How desperate do you have to be to cry out from your pain for help? How long will others have to pray for you until you pray for help? When will you listen to Jesus' voice and surrender all to Him?

At the End of This Week...

Take a couple of days and write down a few things you have learned this week:

- *About Yourself...*
- *About God...*
- *About one way you need to change...*

Final Word - *From Death to Life—Rise UP!*

I close with this summary:

If He is all for us, we need not fear what man can do unto us. God will deliver us, either from death or in death. We must trust, please and obey God rather than man; at times, we will suffer because we choose not to sin and go the way of the world. We will not be moved but anything or anyone. We will keep focused on God.

> *"Faith is taking the first step even when you don't see the whole staircase."*
> -Martin Luther

Say and do this: **My passionate faith empowers me to do the good works God created me to do in Christ.**

These BOYZ Resisted. They feared God, not man. They trusted God's outcome for their life than the outcome of man. Don't let man or society dictate how you should live and who you should serve. Have a personal relationship with God and He will be there for you in time of trouble. You will live, you will not die.

Shot full of bullets and nearing death, God gave me a second chance to RISE UP. I say to you...

Rise up from fear and being the walking dead to new life in Christ.

Rise up to seize the moment and claim your destiny in Christ.

Rise up from the grave of pleasing yourself and others to pleasing God.

RISE UP!

About the Author

J acob Lopez was born and raised in Bronx, NY. By his loving parents Pedro and Rose Lopez. Growing up in the Bronx wasn't easy and he lost his purpose and joined a gang which almost led to death but God came and turned it around for the good.

Today, Jacob is a loving husband, a father of two wonderful children. He is passionate about teaching the God's Word and loves to see people transformed and living life with a purpose. He takes the time to mentor young adults and men in a ministry called "The Brotherhood". Jacob also volunteers in a program called "Casa Refugio" (translated means House of Refuge) for men who overcome drug addiction.

Jacob has been blessed to serve as an Associate Pastor at Koinonia House of Worship and the privilege of going around different places sharing his story. Remember everyone has a past the key is what will you do to start a new chapter.

For more information please visit: www.pastorjacoblopez.com or fb.com/jacobIsrael.lopez

Endnotes

1 http://christian-quotes.ochristian.com/
   Intercession-Quotes/

2 https://www.goodreads.com/author/
   quotes/1114699.Henry_Cloud

CPSIA information can be obtained
at www.ICGtesting.com
Printed in the USA
BVOW10s0303180817
492405BV00018B/216/P